This Self-Love Book Belongs to:

_____

_____

I am calm and relaxed in all situations.

My muscles are relaxed.

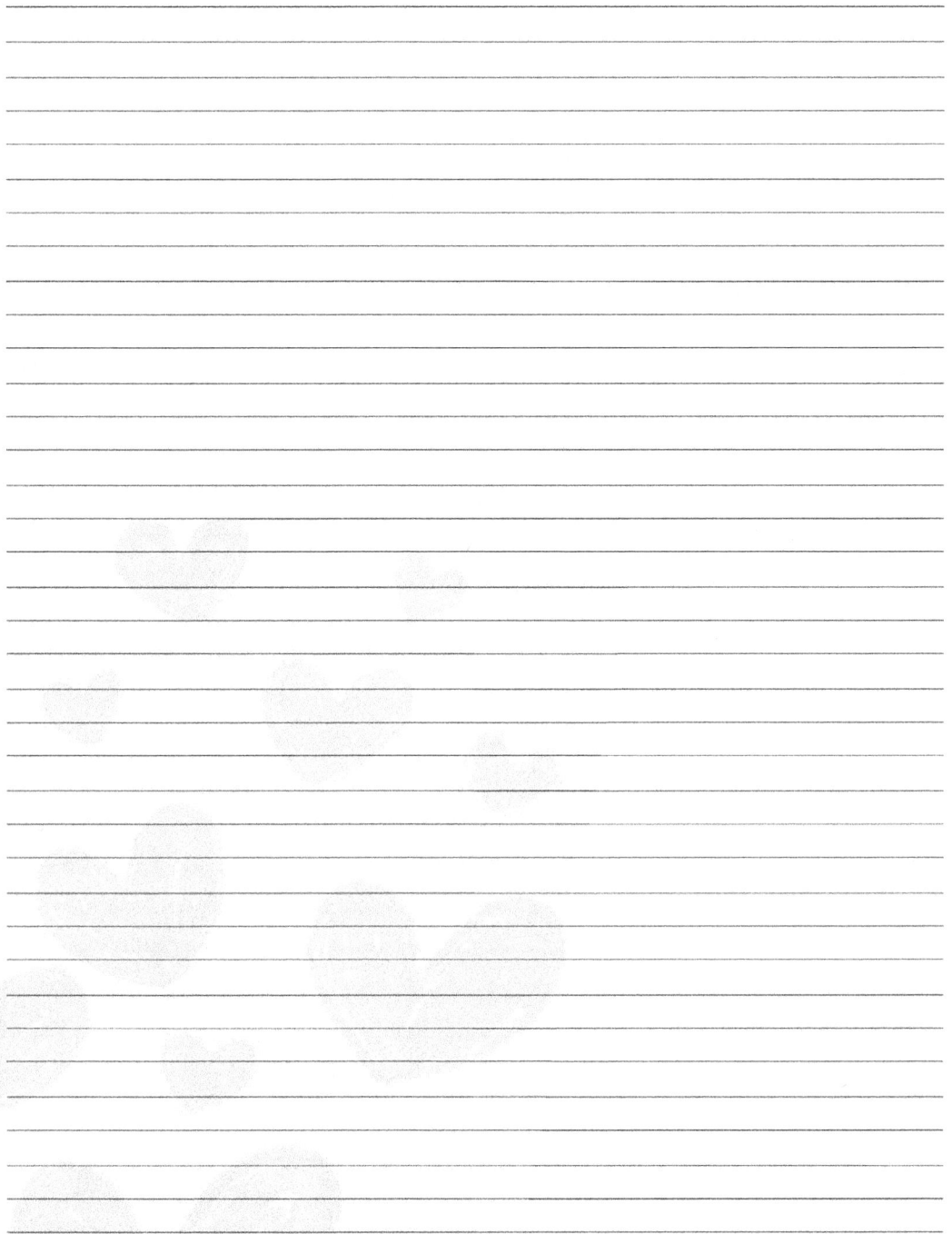

My tension is melting away.

I am relaxed and calm.

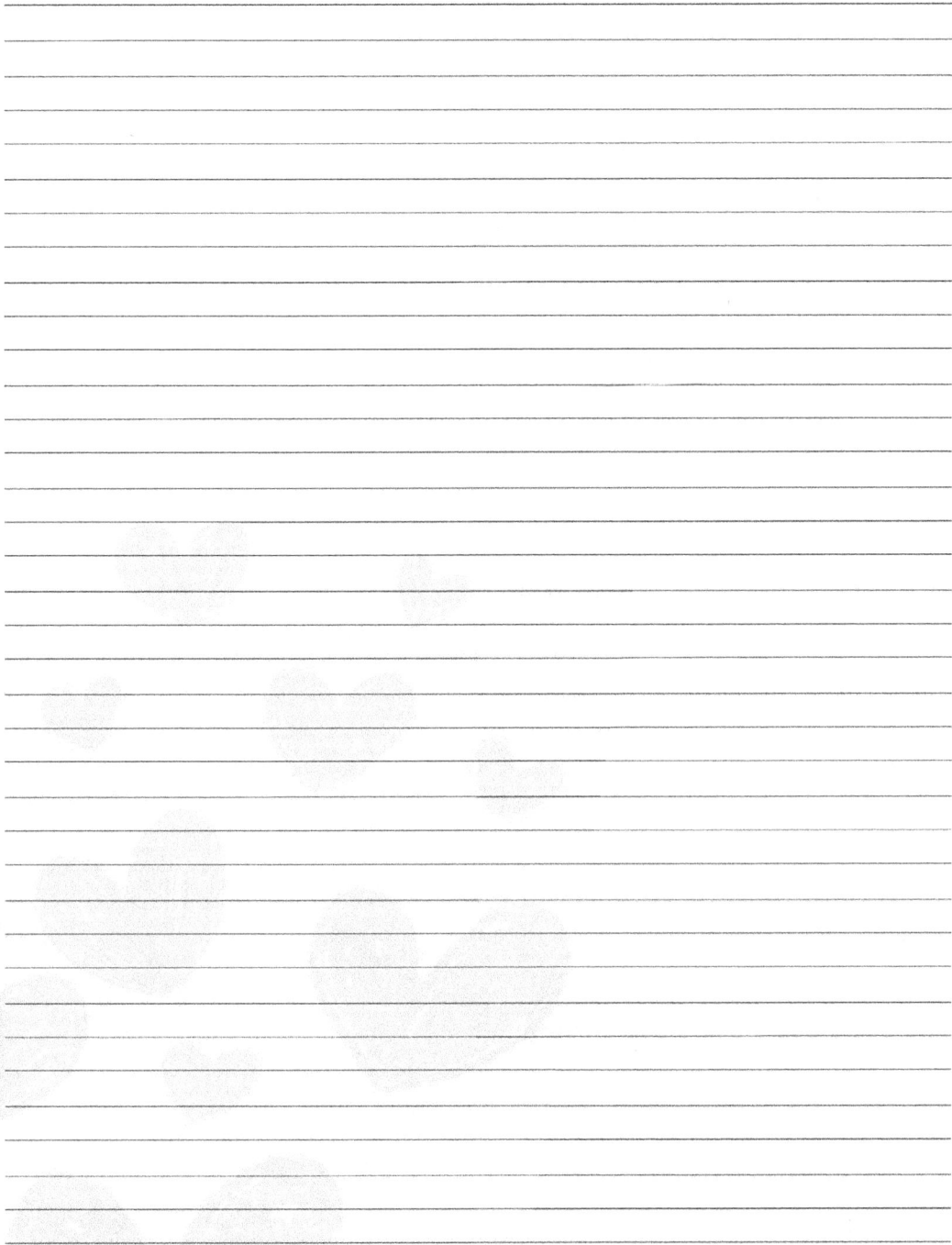

I am comfortable around other people.

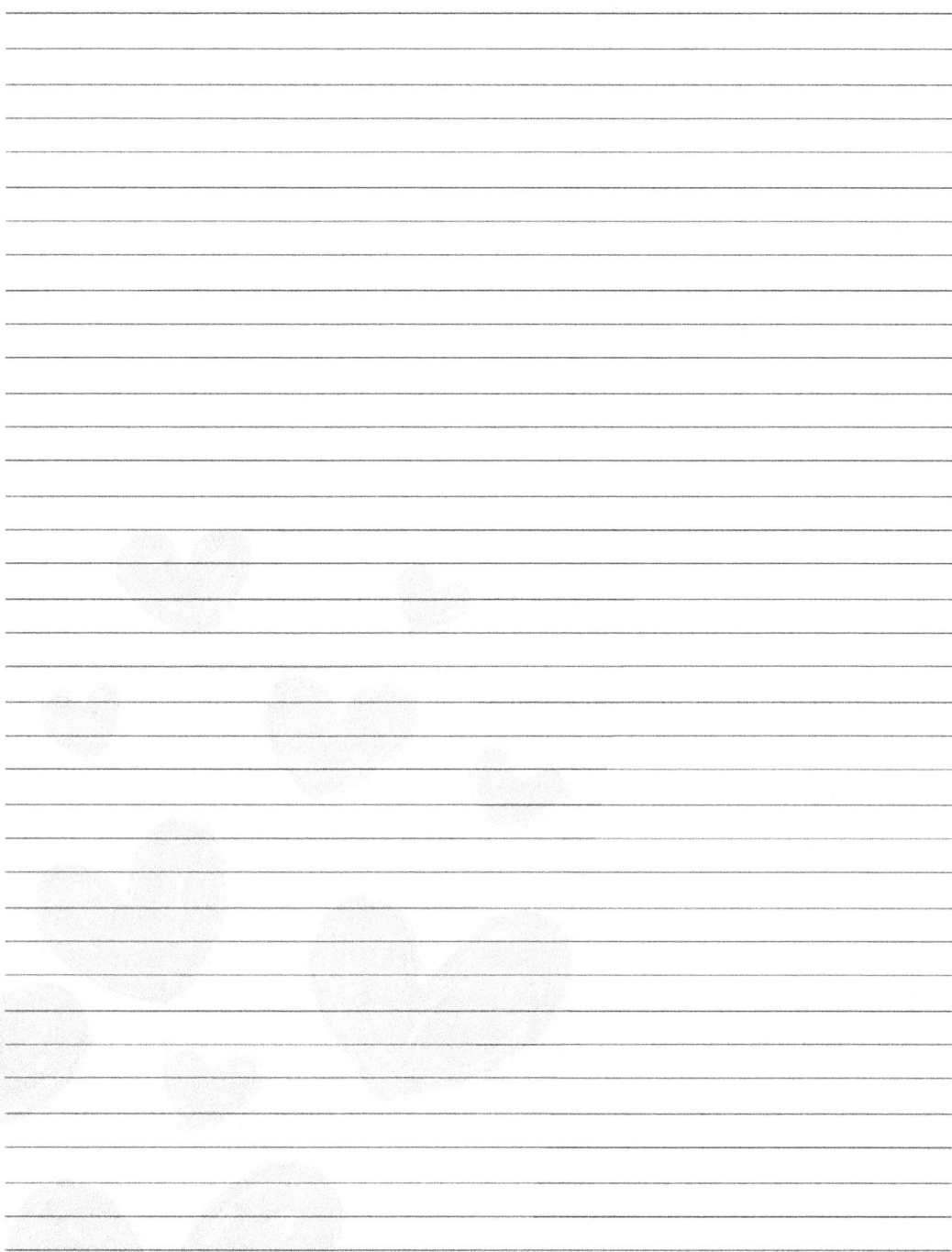

I am thankful and grateful for the good in my life.

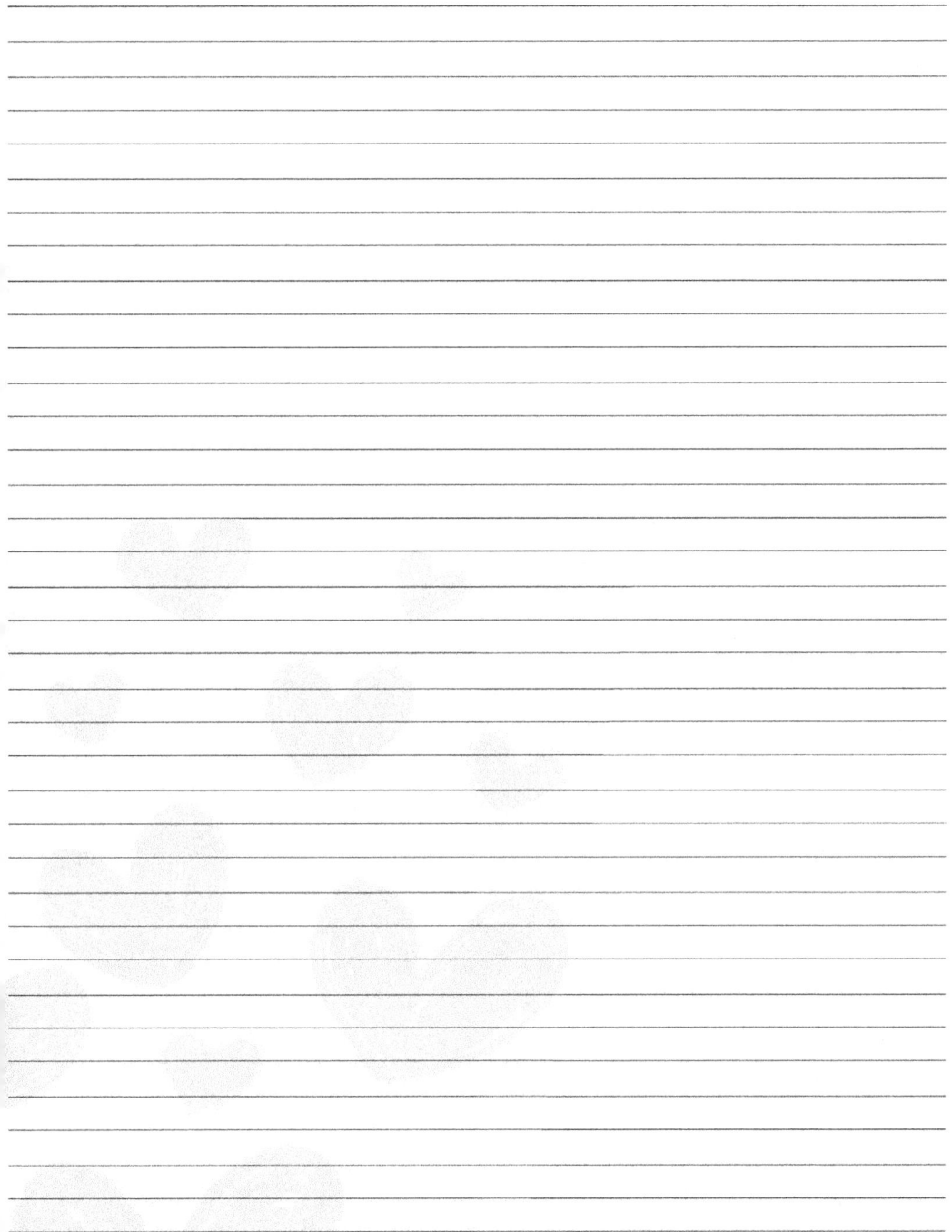

Calmness washes over me with every deep breath I take.

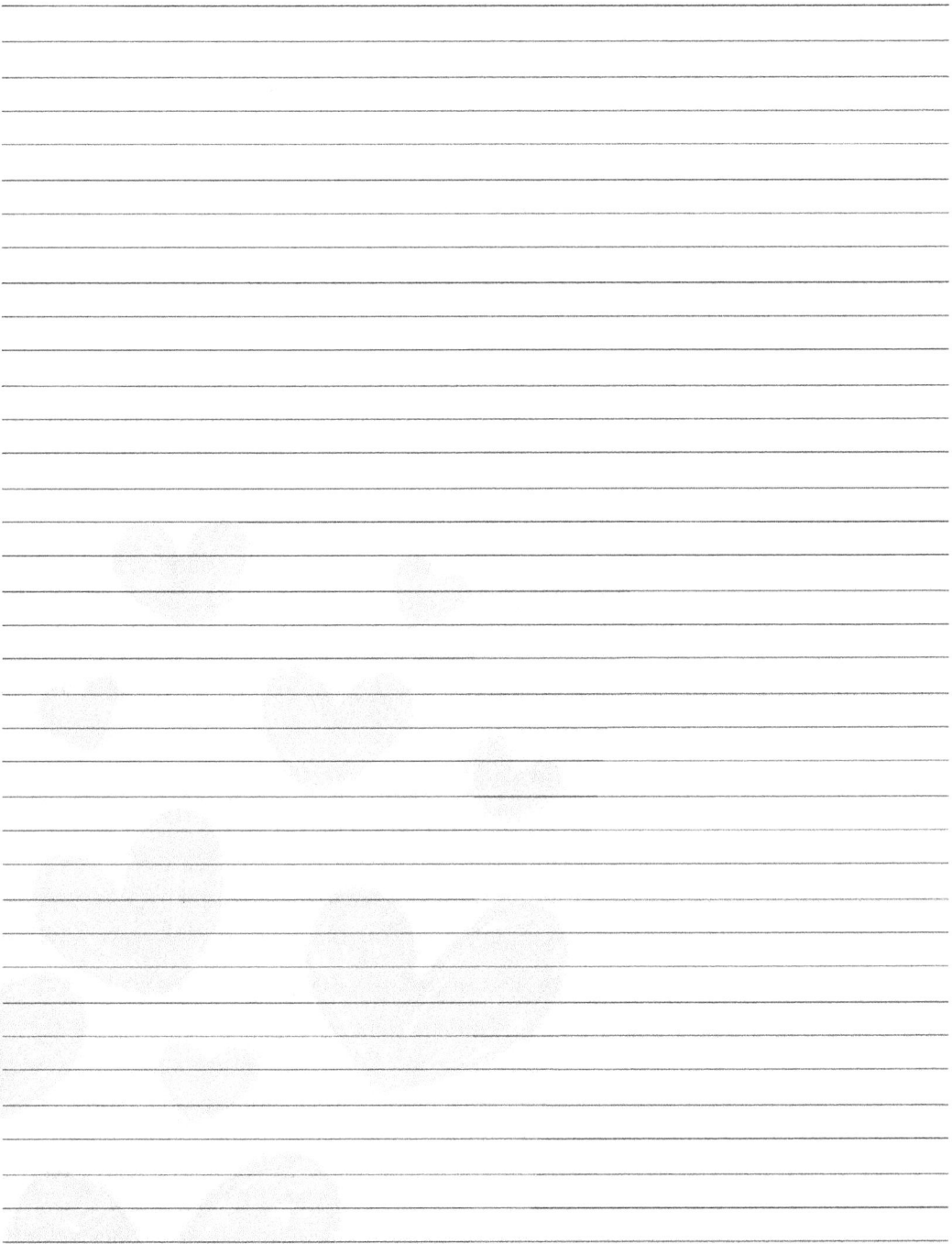

I am releasing all negative emotions from my system.

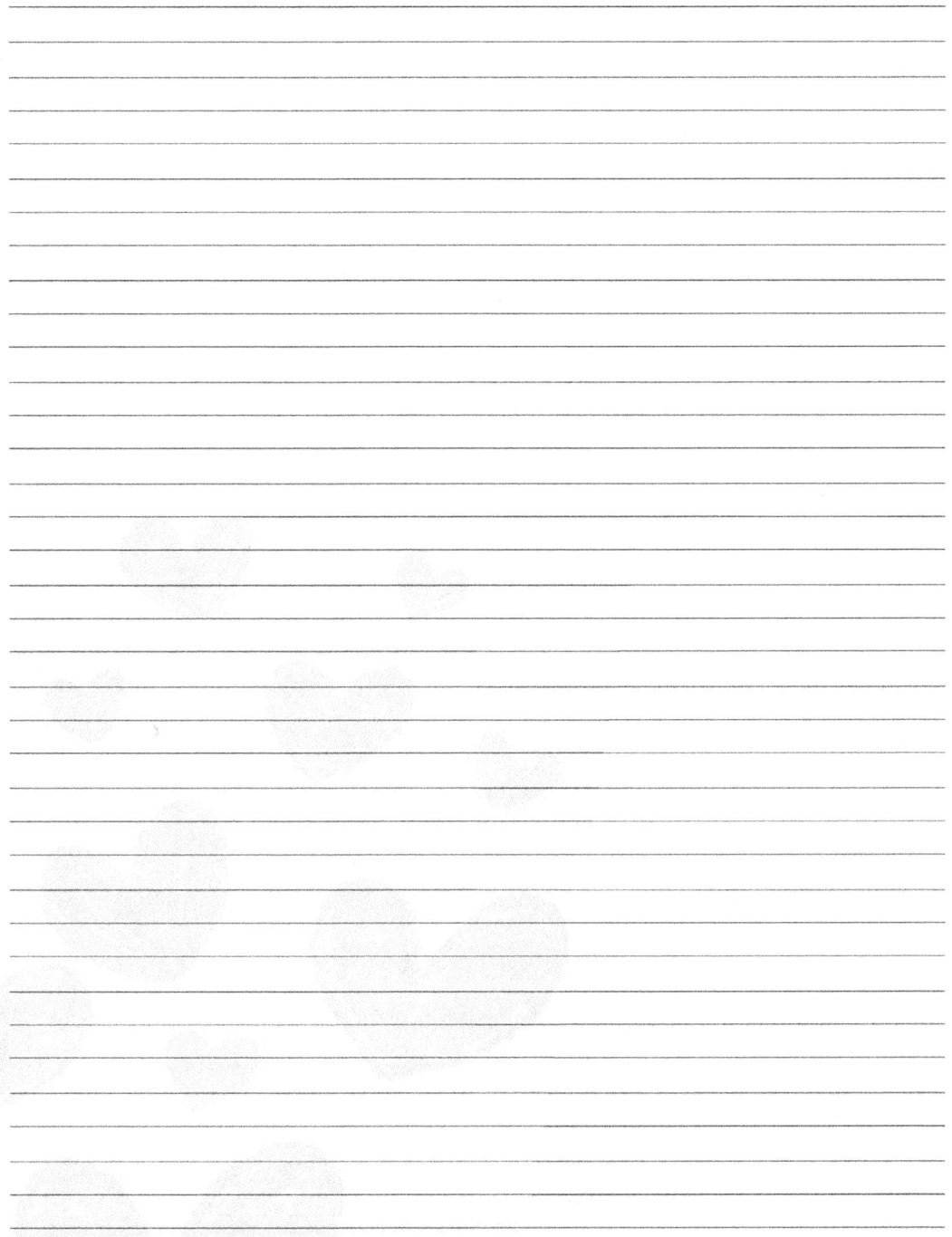

I deserve a peaceful and loving life.

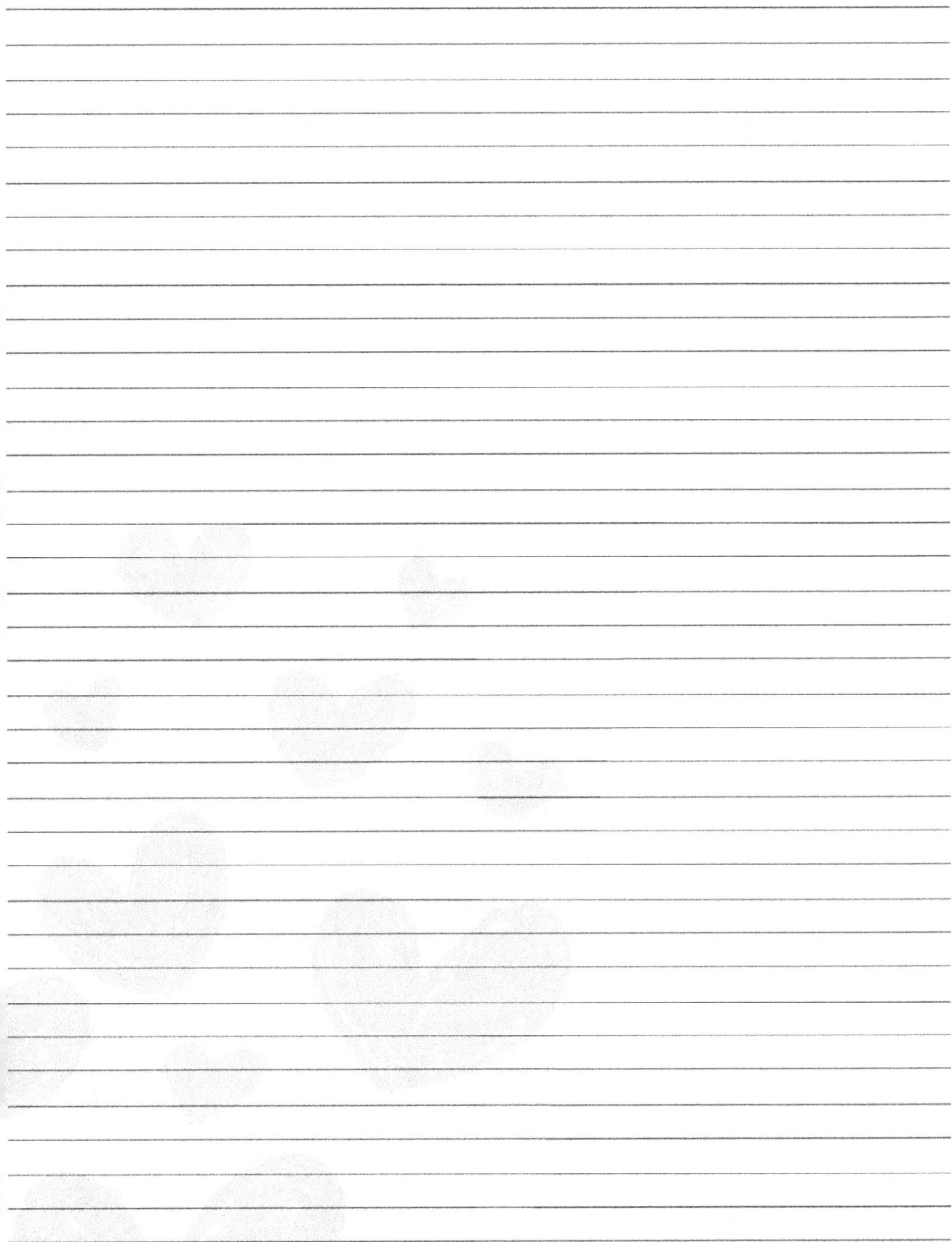

I am breathing slowly and deeply, filling myself with calmness.

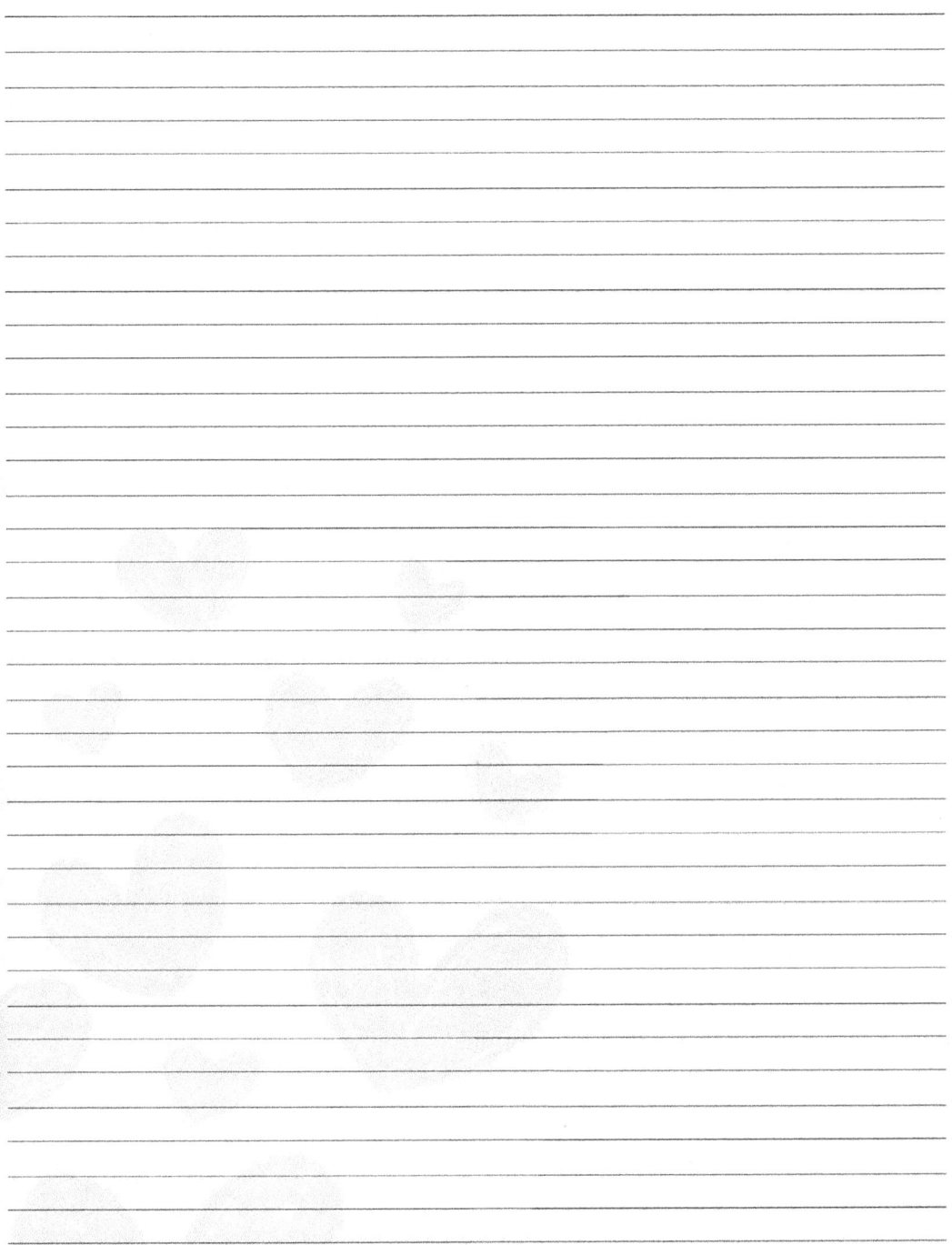

I am letting go of all my worries and fears.

I deserve happiness and joy.

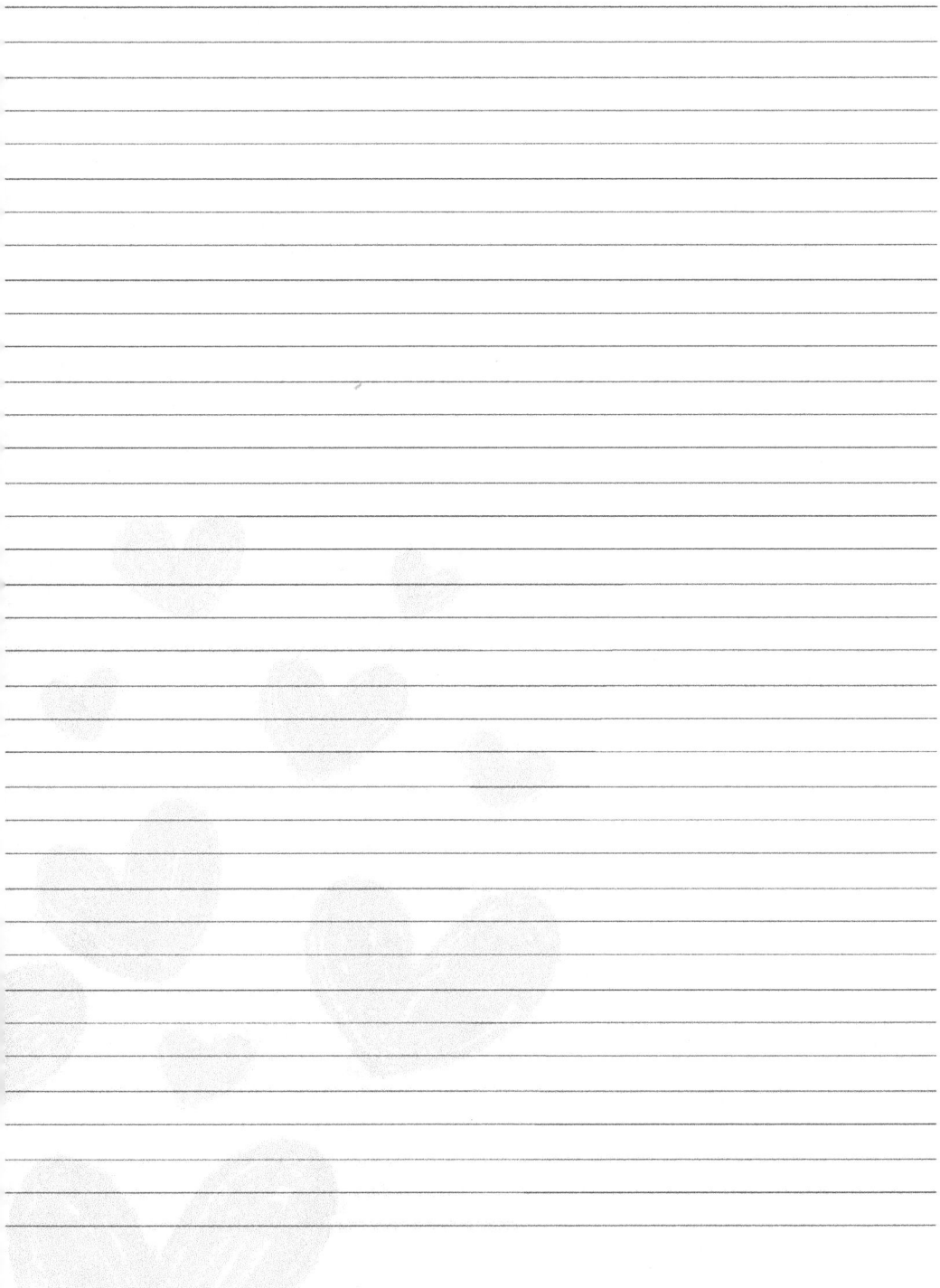

I am calm and at ease.

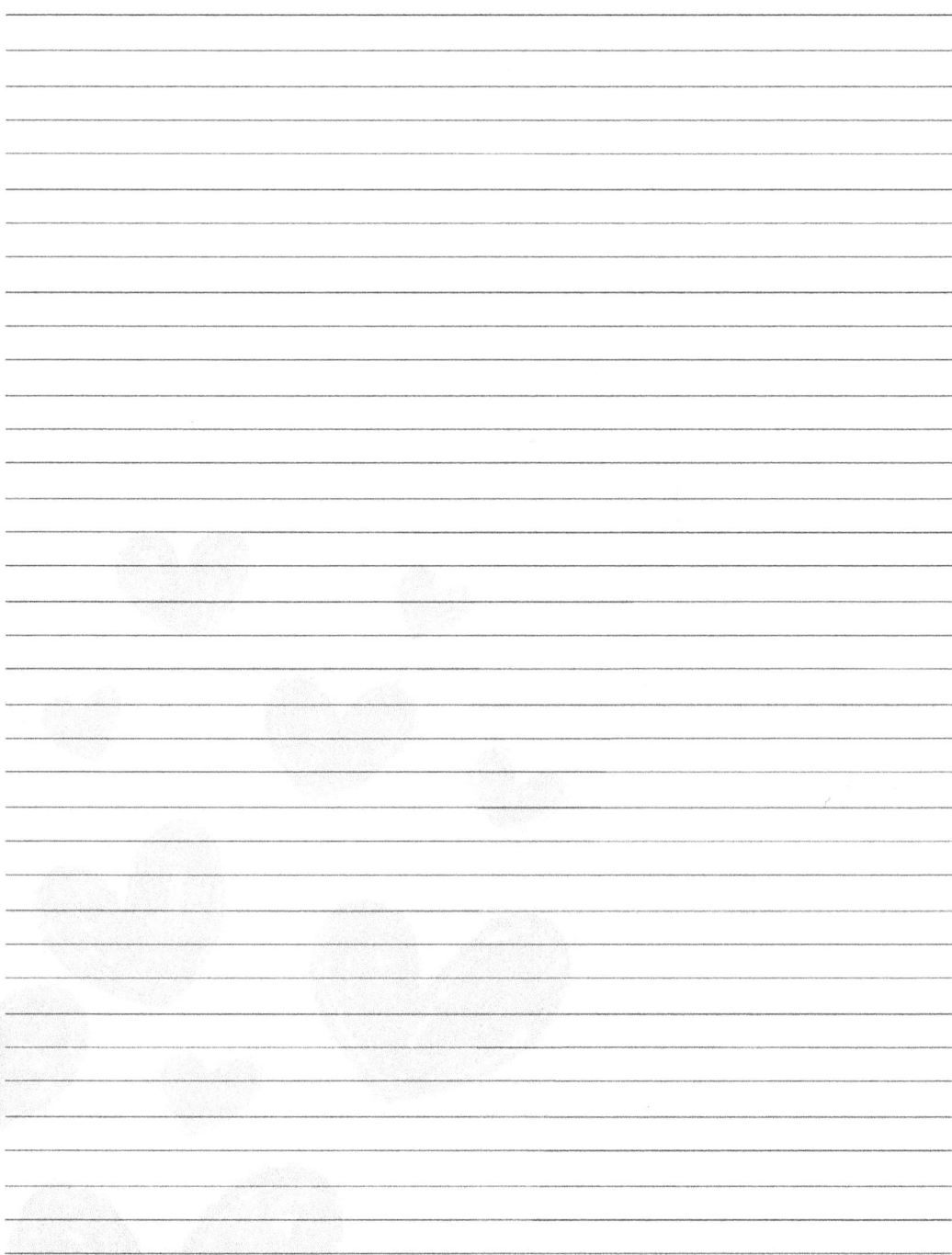

I surround myself with peace and pleasant emotions.

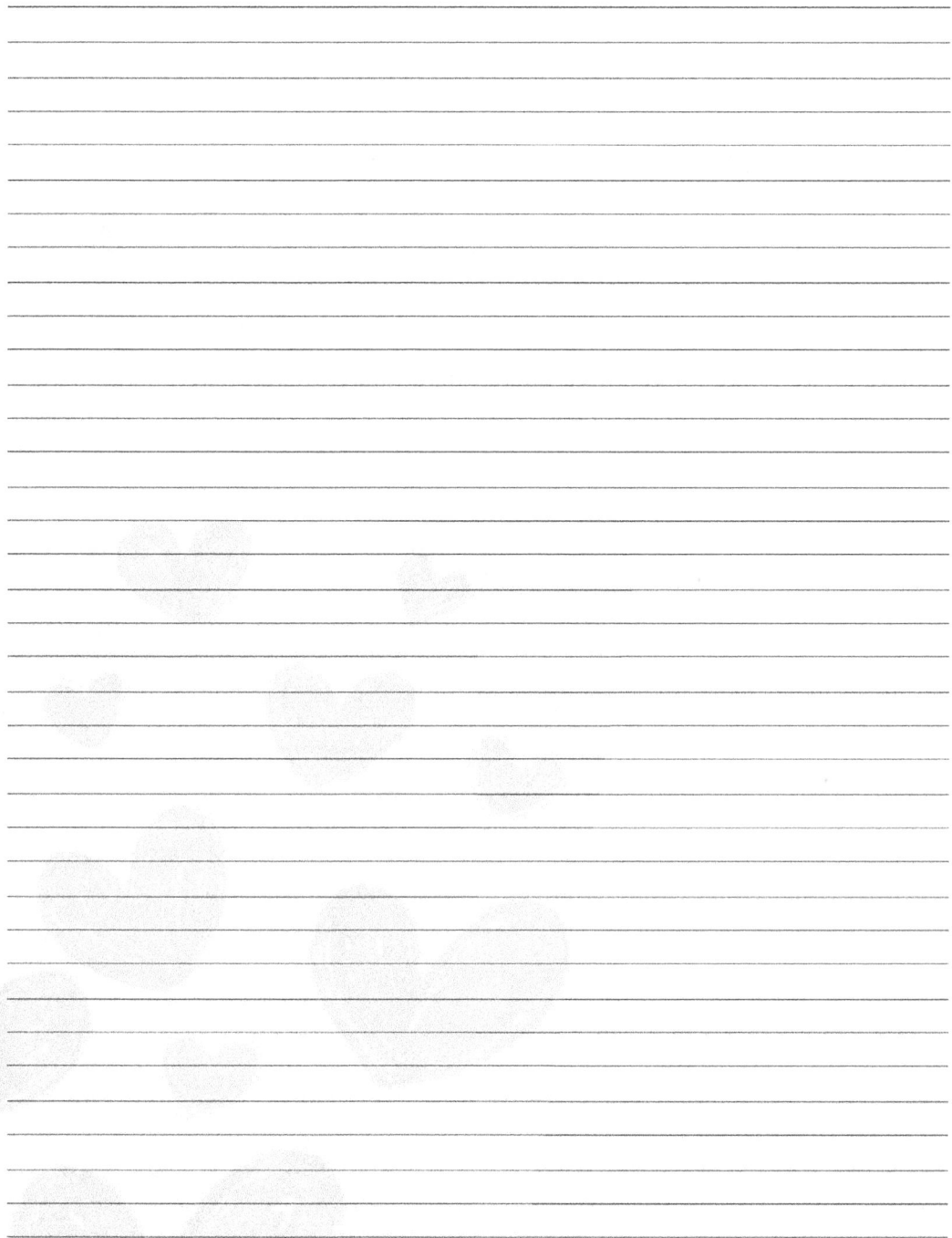

I choose to move my focus on happy experiences.

Despite how I feel, I understand this feeling and situation are temporary.

Serenity, tranquillity, and other pleasurable emotions engulf my being.

My thoughts are slowing down.

My breathing is anchored from within my core and
this breathing is relaxing to my body and mind.

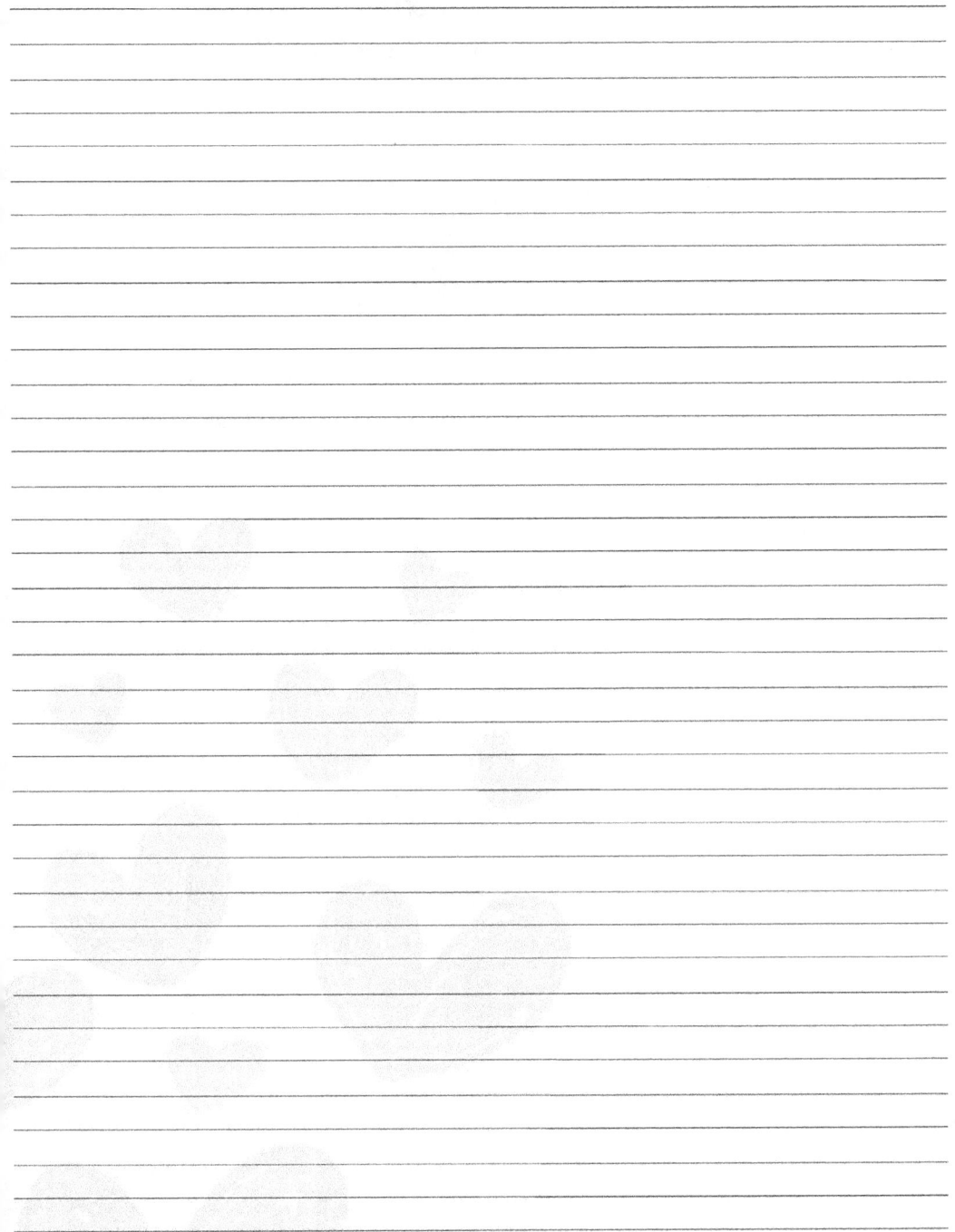

As my body and mind become more relaxed,
I can problem-solve more effectively.

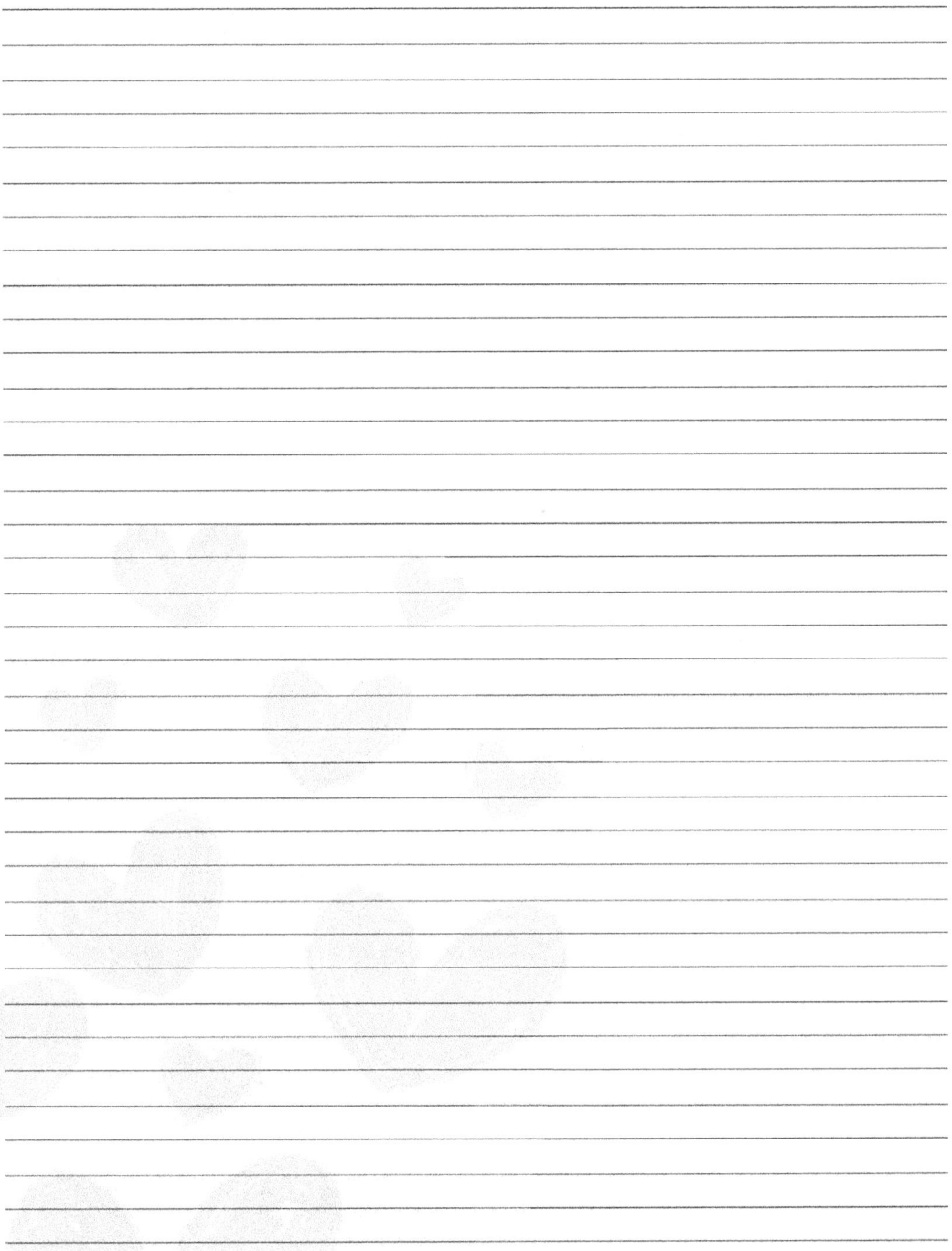

One day at a time, one step at a time.

Everything is going to be okay.

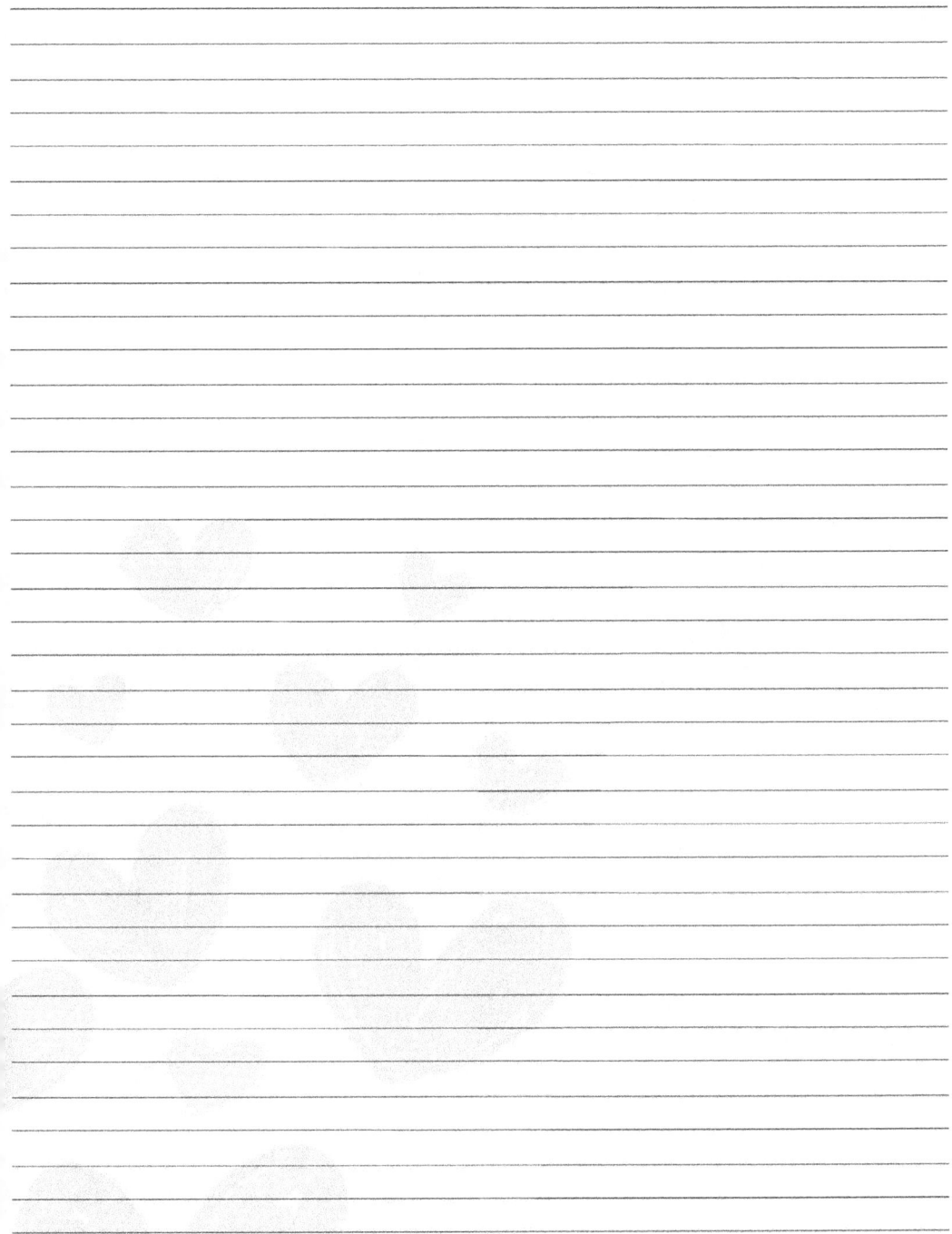

I trust the Universe is looking out for my higher good.

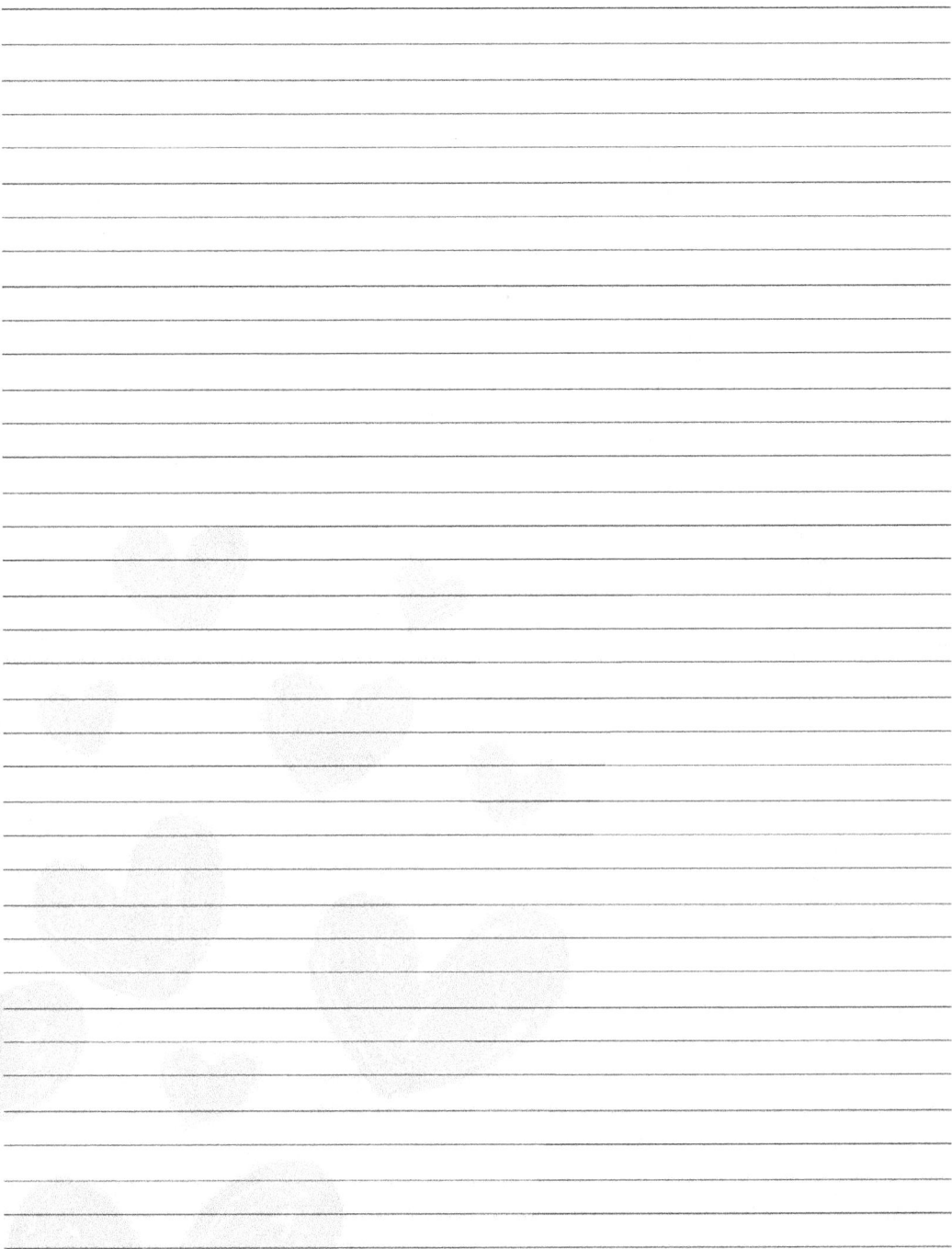

I am in harmony and balance with life.

I choose to feel peaceful.

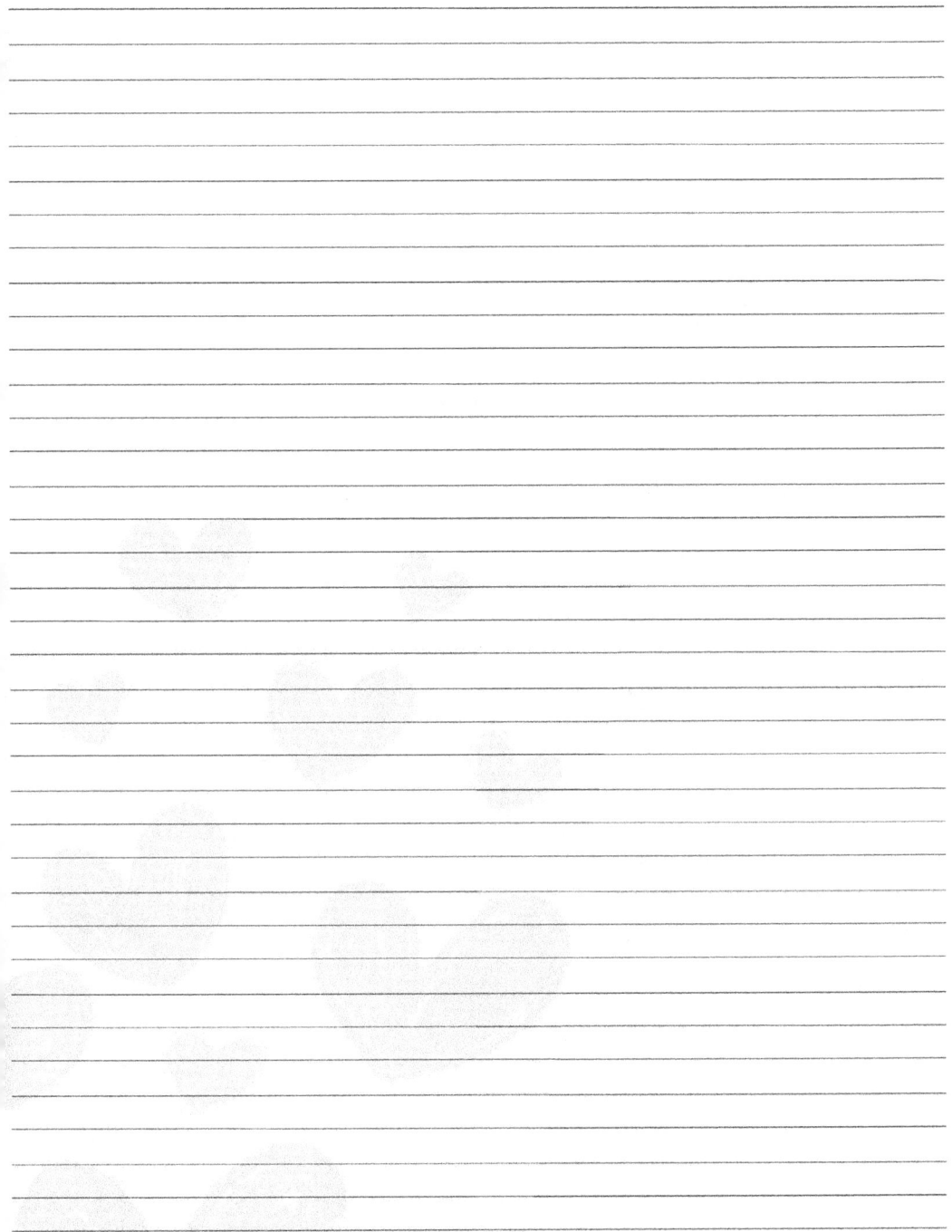

Good things continually happen to me.

I have endless strength.

I have the power to face any difficulty.

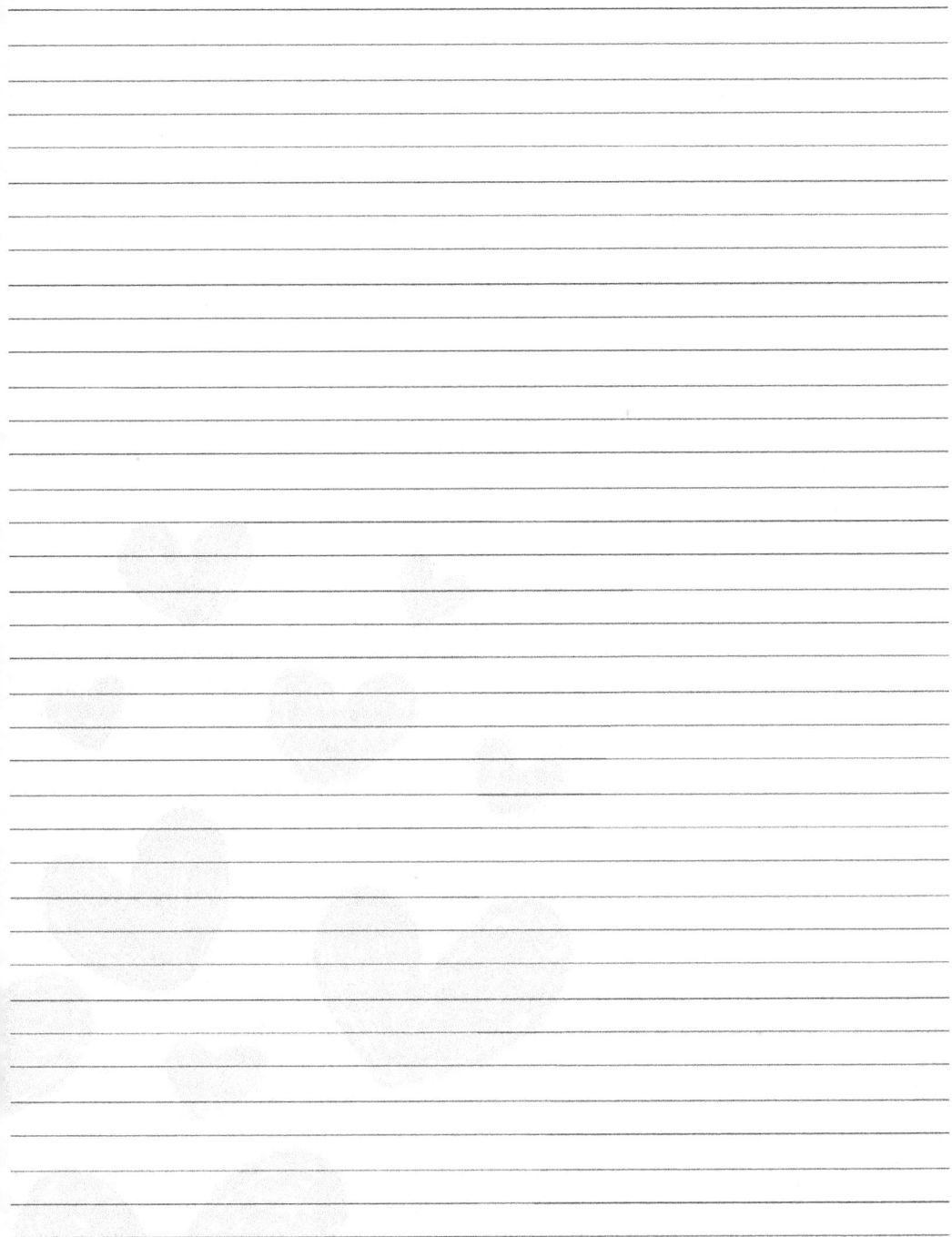

I am in control of my thoughts.

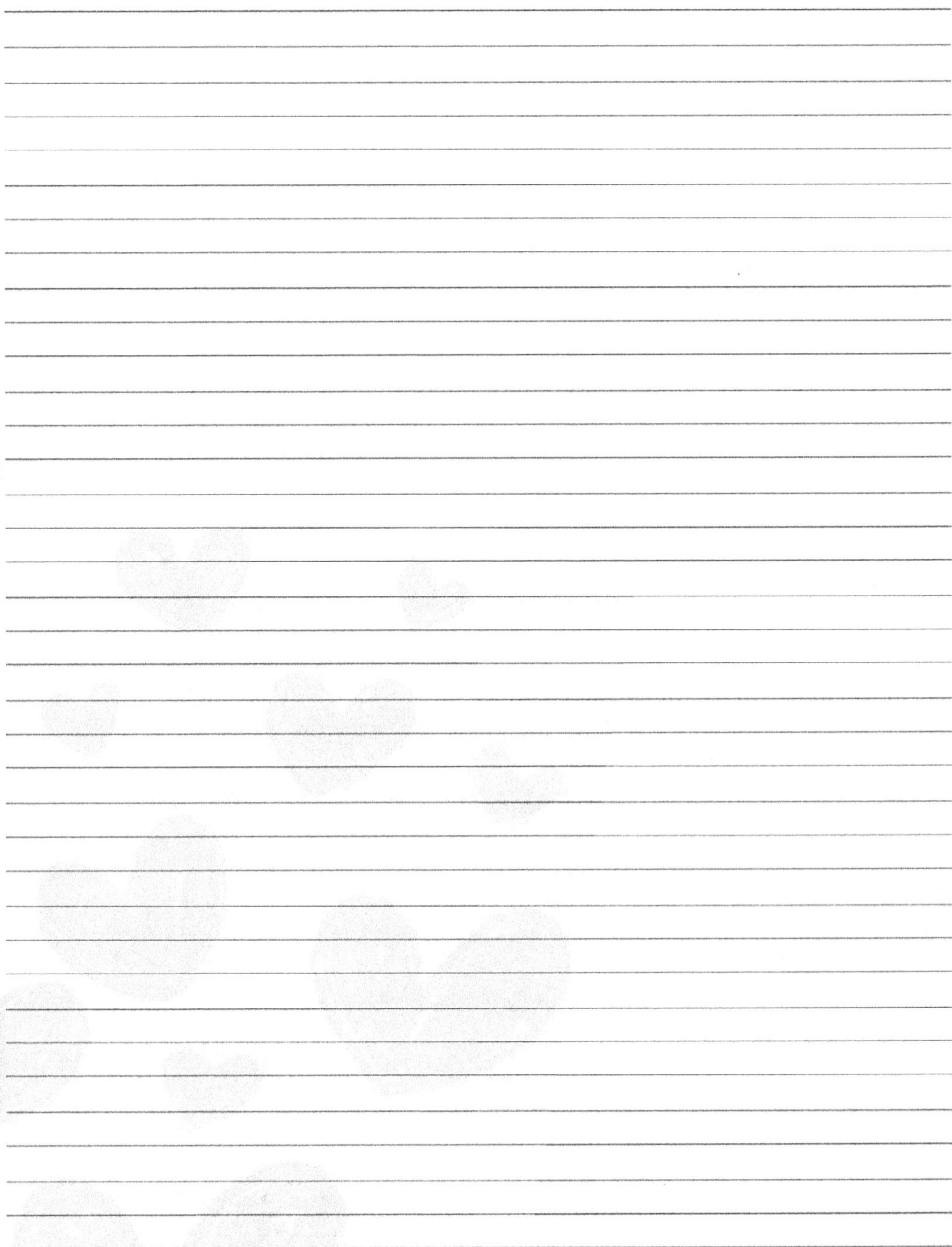

I am at home in my body.

I make the decisions for myself.

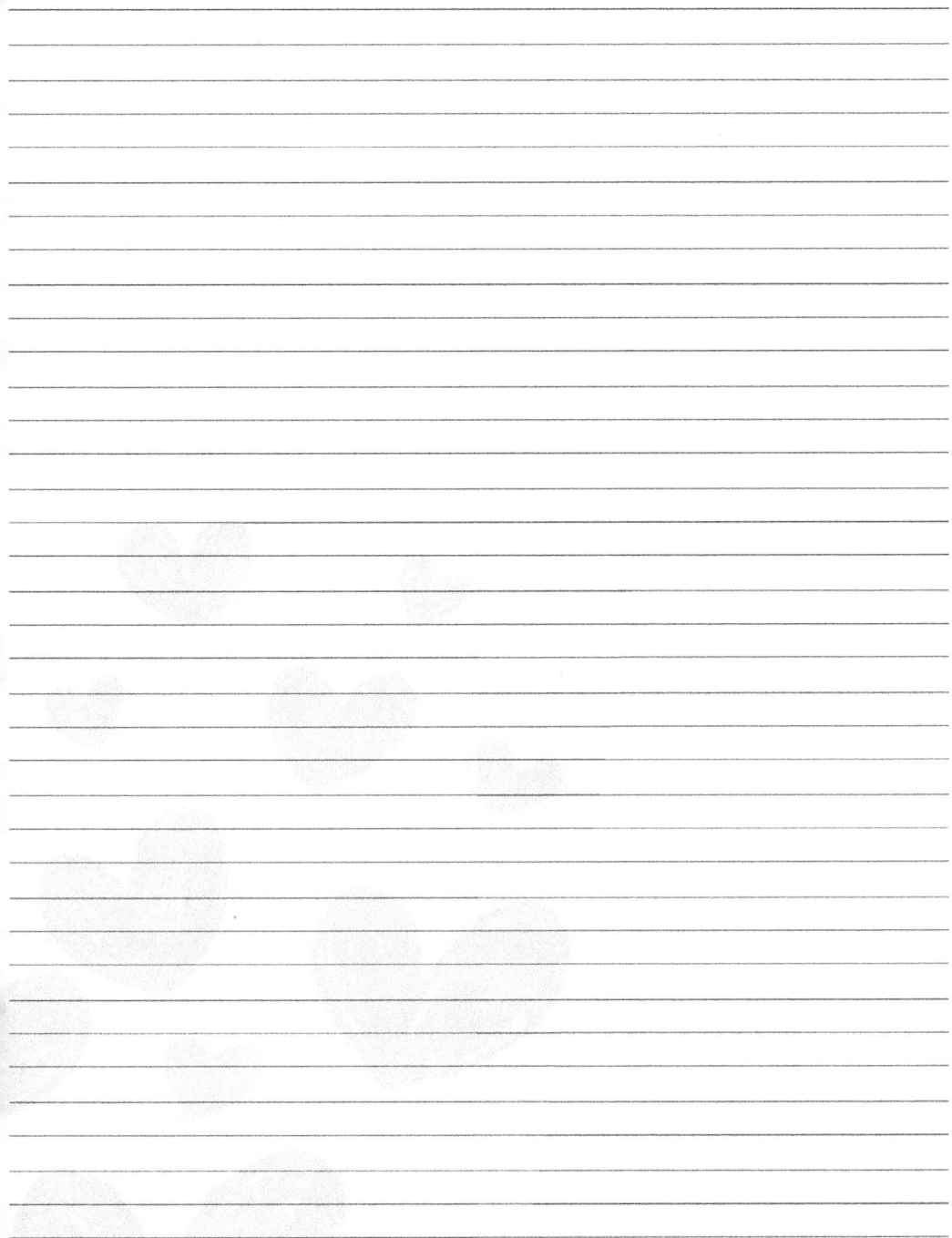

My happy thoughts help create my healthy body.

I am worthy of good experiences.

Every situation is easy for me to handle.

I am capable.

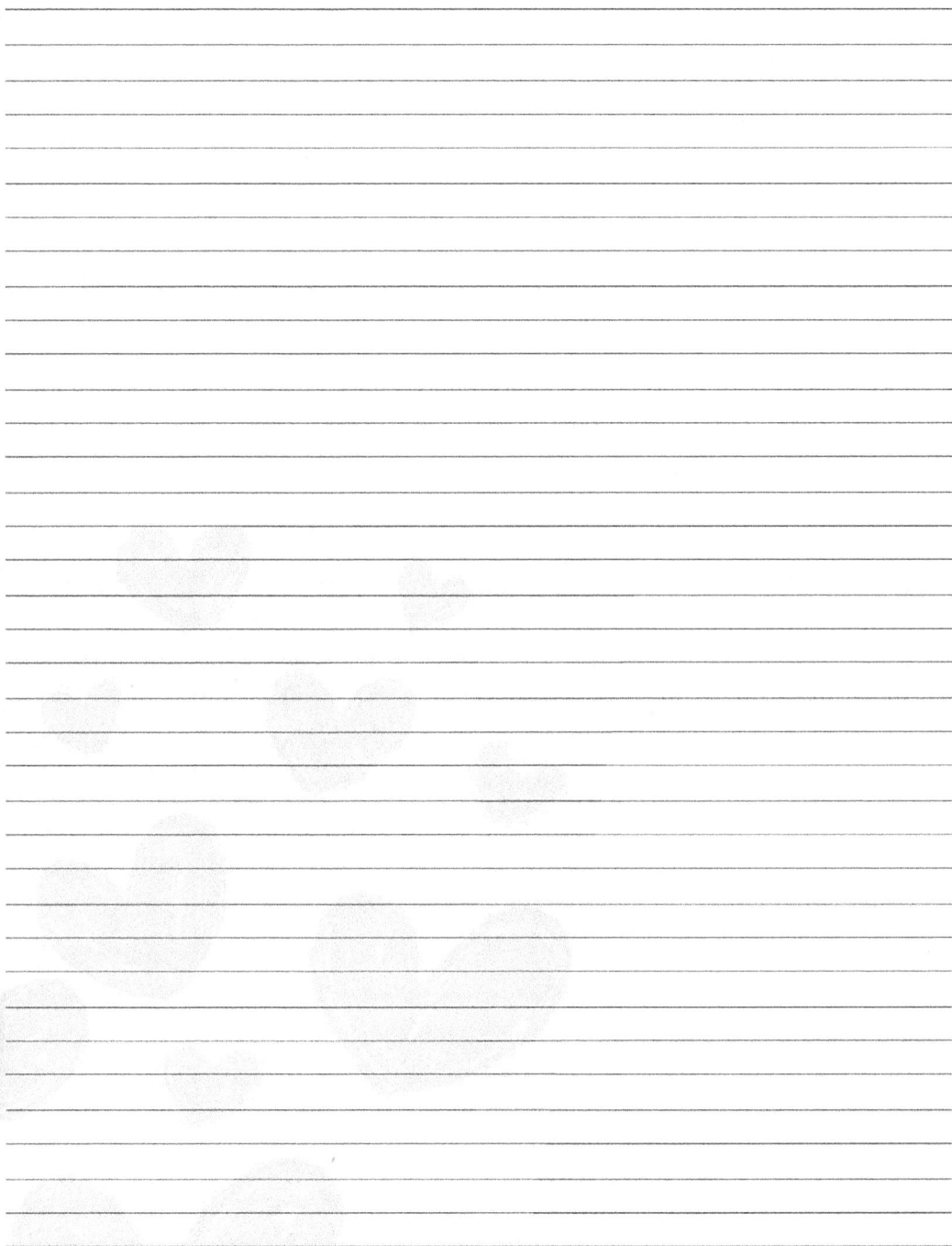

I am safe at this very moment.

The truth is I am blessed, loved, and supported.

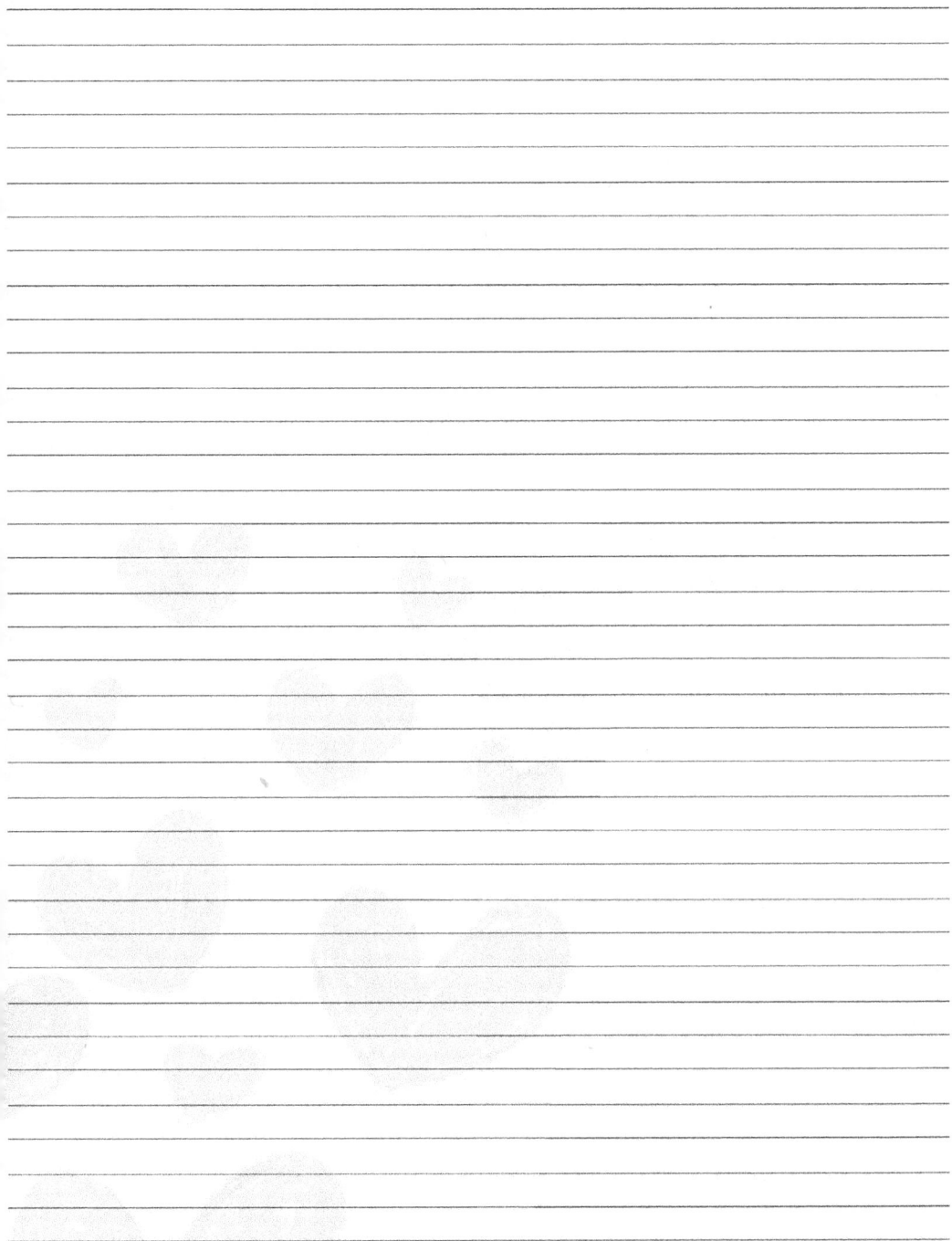

Life is always working for me.

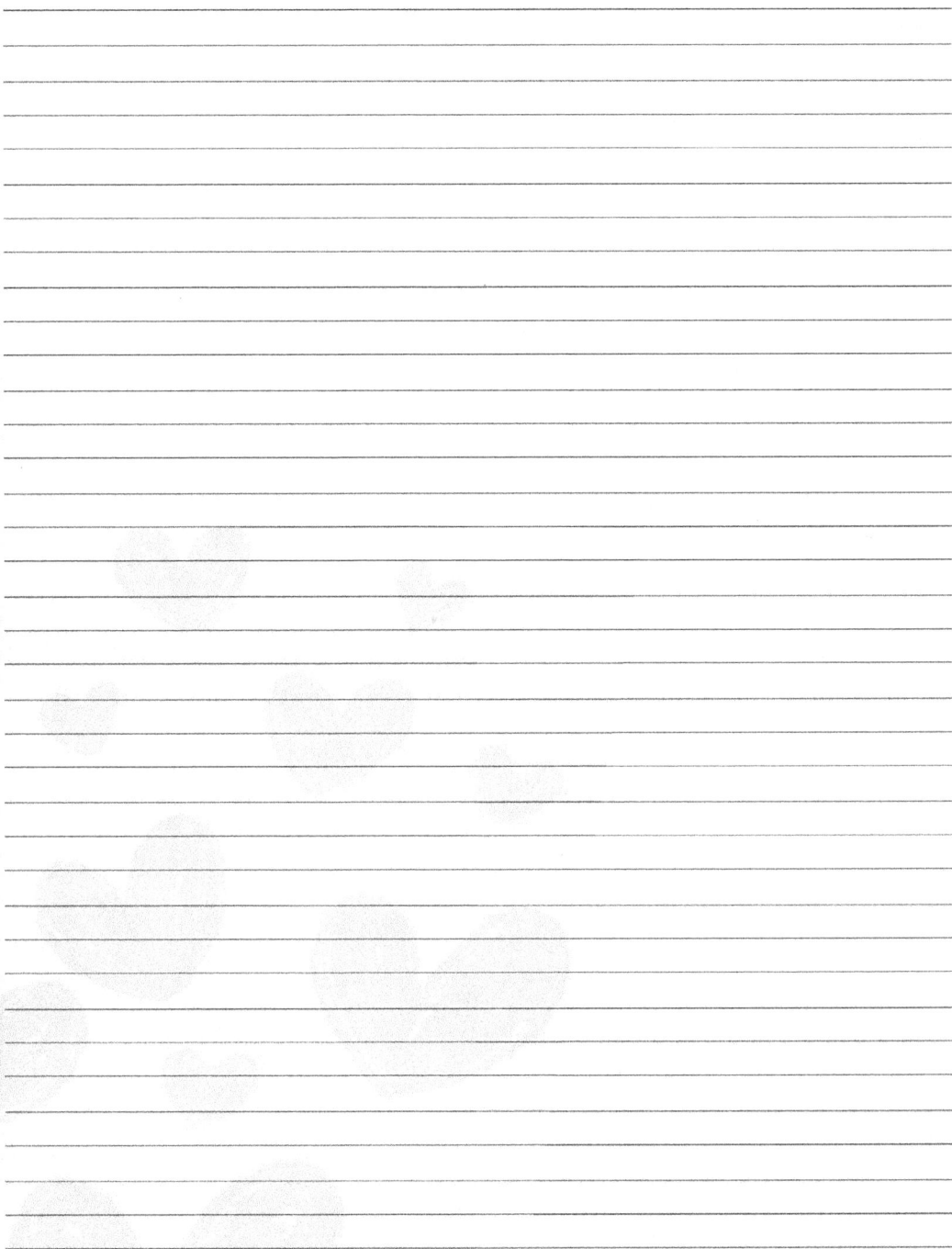

I am safe and in control.

I have the ability to overcome setbacks.

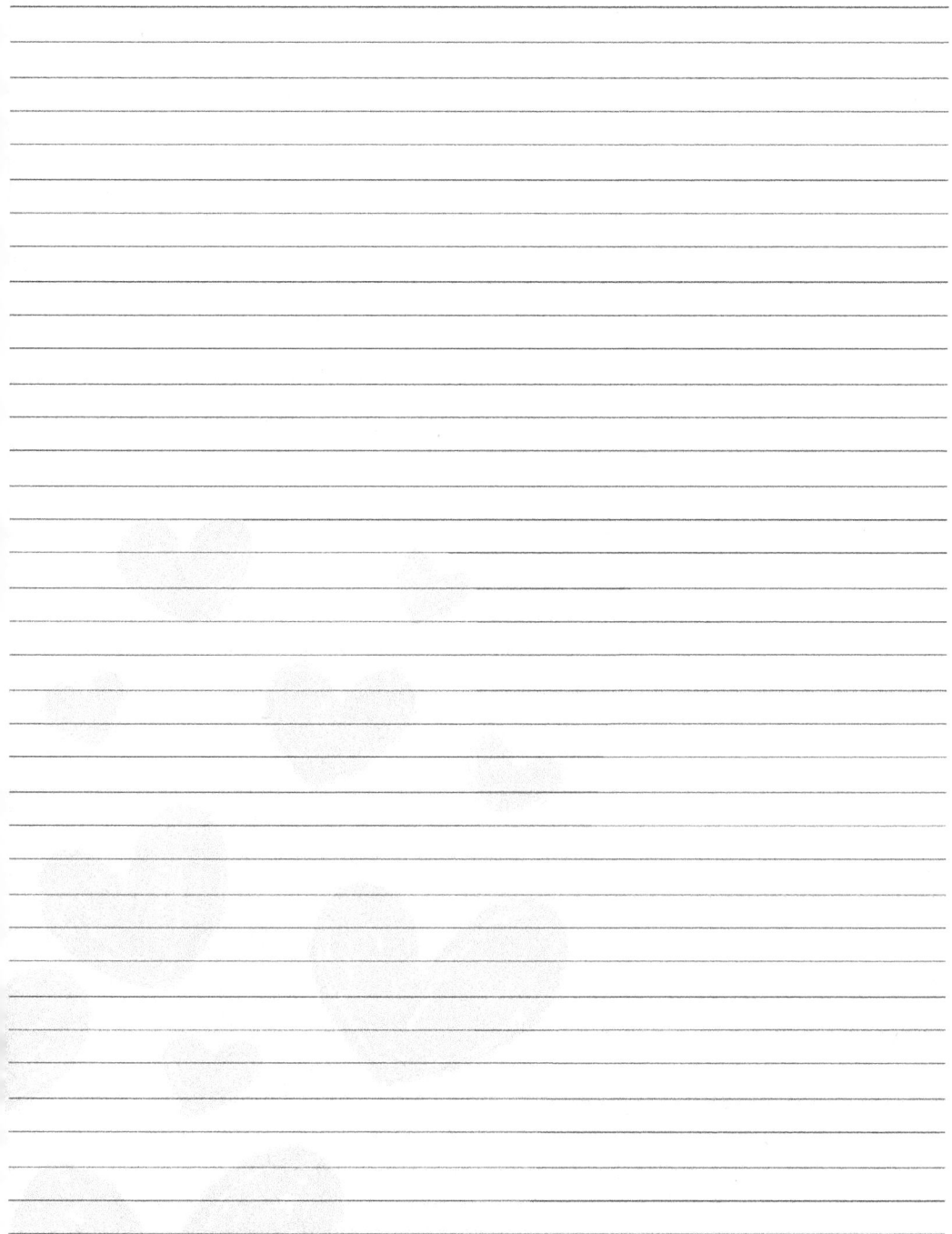

I am blessed, loved, and supported.

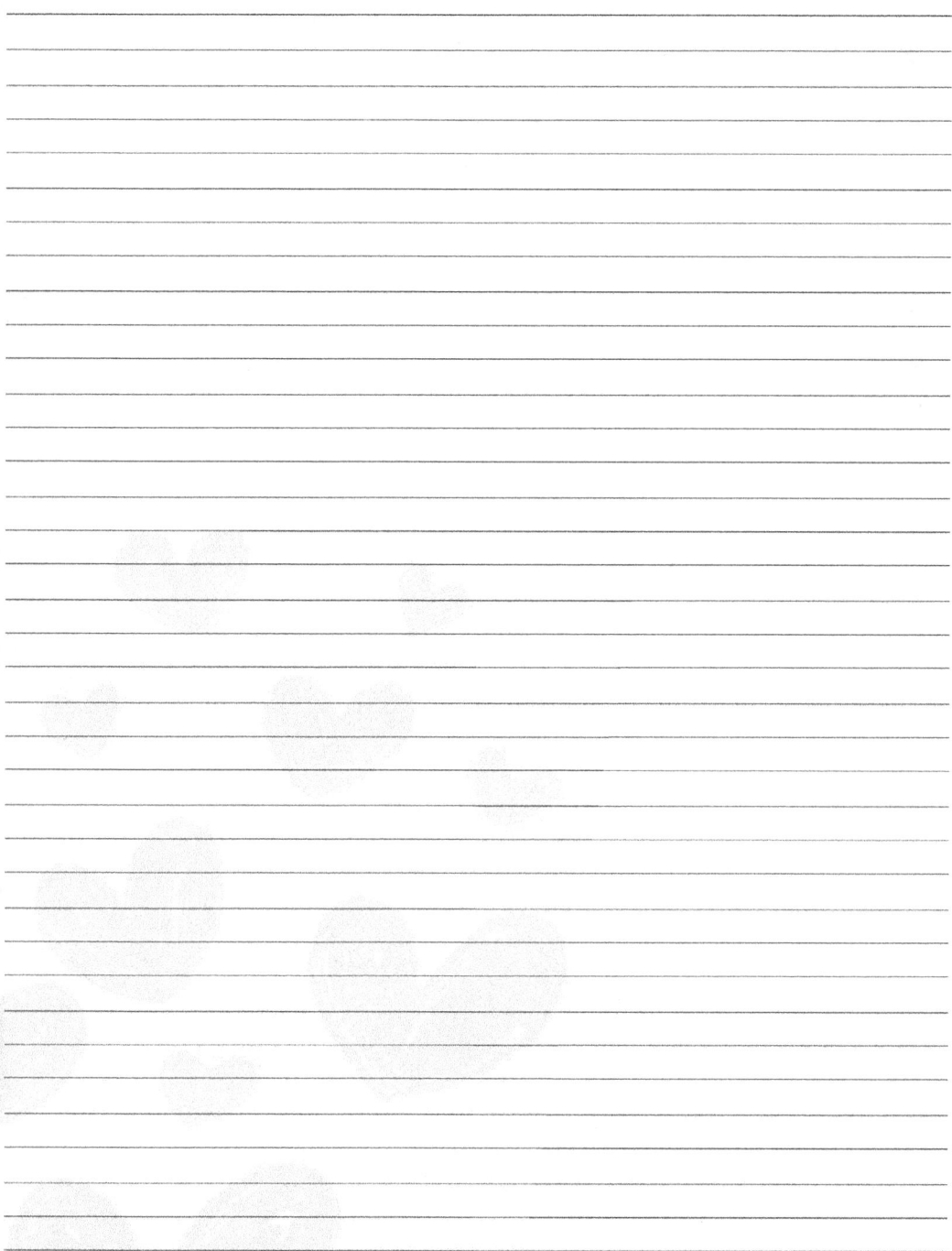

I accept myself and bring peace to my mind and heart.

I believe in myself here and now!

I am healing.

I love myself.

I am worthy of good things.

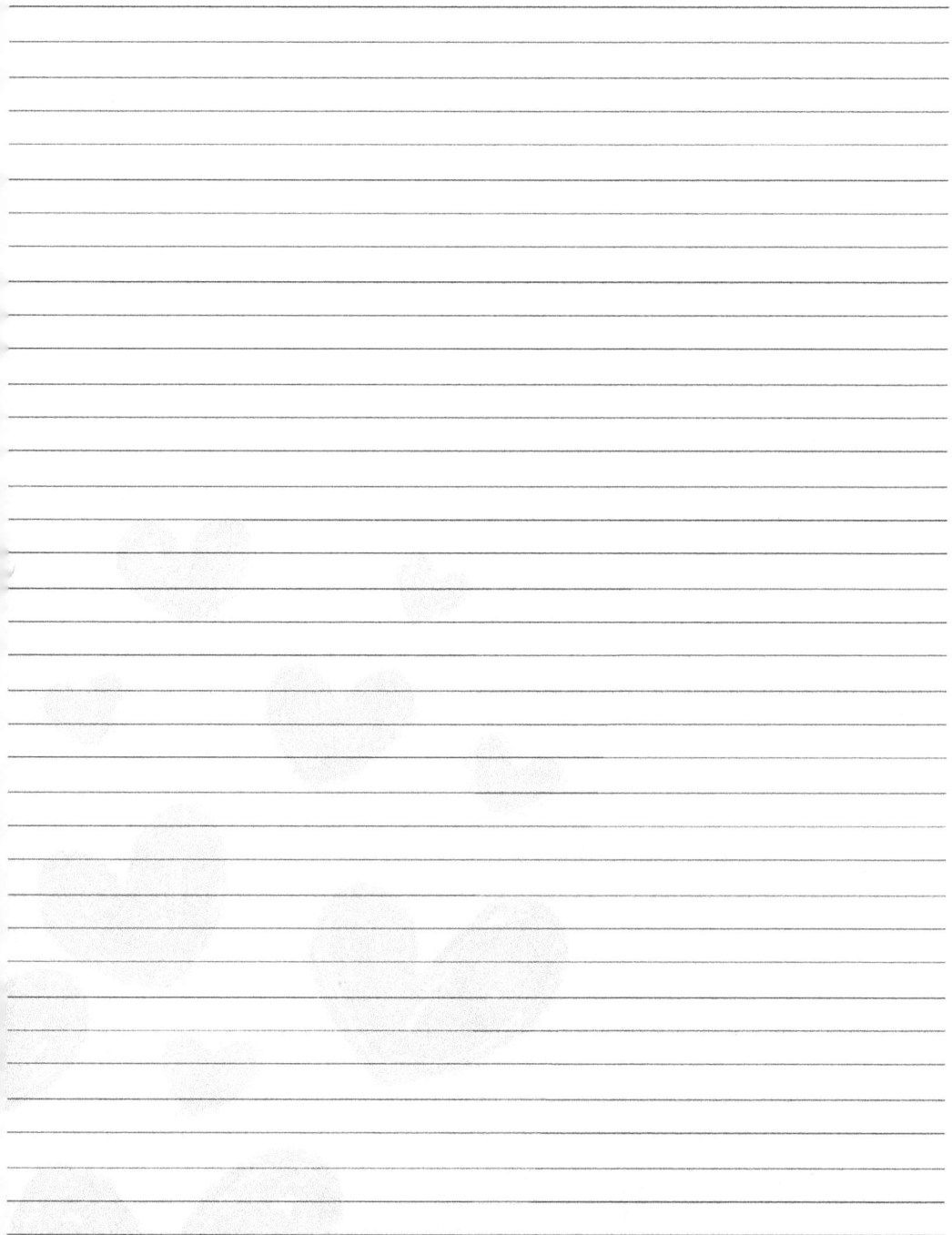

I respect myself and treat myself with kindness and love.

I have all that I need to get through this day.

I am attracting positive healing energy to myself.

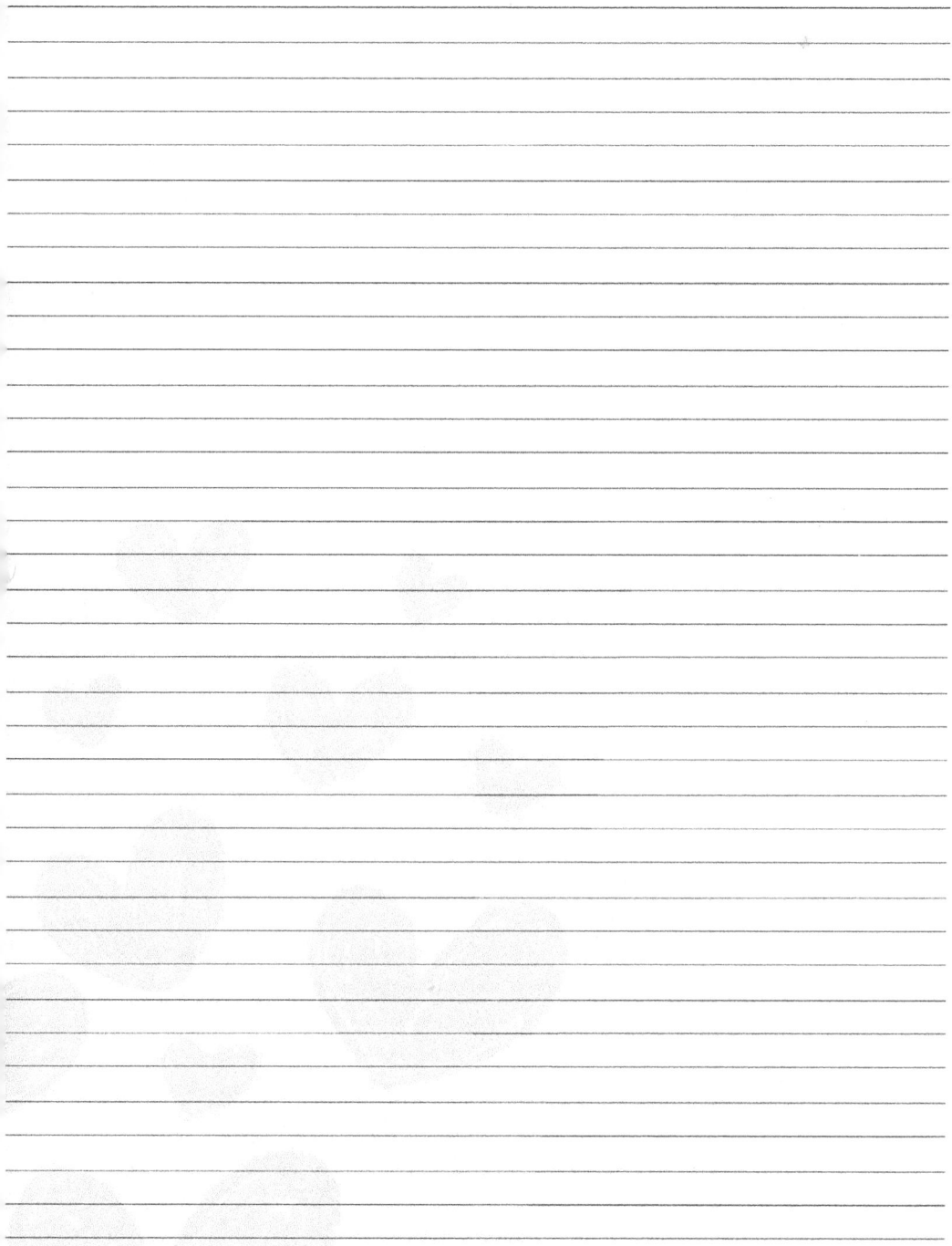

No part of this book may be reproduced
without written permission from the author